D0866409

DOGS

DOGS

ARIEL BOOKS

**Andrews McMeel
Publishing**

Kansas City

ISBN: 0-8362-3017-5

Library of Congress Catalog Card Number: 91-77092

Table of Contents

⚊⚫⚬ Introduction ⚬⚫⚊

Thousands of years ago, in the mists of prehistory, humankind made friends with the dog. For the first time, humans encountered another being they neither ate nor got eaten by. The friendship formed that far-off day continues to flourish.

The relationship between human beings and canines has always been unique. No two species have formed such a close and mutually necessary bond. Other animals have been domesticated, of course. But none have ever worked so closely with humans—helping the blind, guarding the home, even playing with the children. Dogs are quite simply humankind's best friend.

Dogs: A History

What gives dogs their cold, wet noses? According to tradition, a dog saved by Noah discovered a leak in the ark. The loyal dog plugged the leak (and saved the ark) by sticking his nose into the hole. This selfless act has chilled the dog's nose forever. . . .

That story may not be true, but it captures the essence of our relationship with dogs. From the earliest days of human history, dogs have been our helpers and friends.

The first dogs to be domesticated were probably wolves trained by prehistoric hunters to help them track game. Hundreds of generations of selective breeding led to the development of the dog breeds we recognize today.

The first book on dogs—called *Hunting With Dogs*—was written more than 2,300 years ago by the Athenian general Xenophon. Later, the Greek historian Arrian wrote a guidebook on the care of hunting dogs. In it, he advises "always pat your Greyhound's head after he catches a hare and say, 'Well done, Cirrus! Well done, Bonnas! Bravo, my Horme!' . . . for like men of generous spirit they love to be praised."

In ancient Egypt, dogs were venerated as symbols of fidelity and watchfulness. It was the Egyptians who first called Sirius the "Dog Star," since that star's appearance on the horizon coincided with the annual floods that made all life along the Nile bloom. What better name for the star signifying annual constancy than "Dog Star"?

Ancient Ethiopians went so far as to select a dog as their king. The royal canine signaled his approval or disapproval of ministers and officers with licks or growls. The dog's will was followed by all.

The Greek mathematician Pythagoras, a firm believer in reincarnation, was also a dog worshiper. When his followers were on their deathbeds, Pythagoras would hold a dog at their mouths, hoping to capture the escaping soul in the animal's body. Pythagoras could imagine no better existence in the next life.

Dogs were bred and kept in the Orient, too. Marco Polo recorded the splendid sight of a hunt under the auspices of the legendary Kublai Khan:

"And when the Prince goes a-hunting, one of these Barons, with his 10,000 men and something like 5,000 dogs, goes toward the right, while the other goes to the left in a like manner. They move along, all abreast of one another, so that the whole line extends over a full day's journey, and no animal can escape them. Truly it is a glorious sight to see the working of the dogs and the huntsmen on such an occasion!"

In medieval Europe, dogs were among the prized possessions of the nobility. They were bred to hunt—and also as pets. Suits of armor for dogs have been carefully preserved; they were custom-made for hunting dogs who pursued wild boar and for larger mastiffs trained to take part in battles. The custom of putting dogs in armor is carried on, to a degree, in the studded collars worn by larger breeds today. "To arme [dogs] agaynst the Woolfe, or other wylde beastes, you may put brode collars about theyr neckes full of nayles, and iron studdes, lyning it with soft leathers within," wrote one medieval dog expert.

Dogs were also bred for fighting. Bull-baiting and bear-baiting — "sports" in which pack dogs would fight the larger, more ferocious animals to the death — were popular up to the Victorian era. (Indeed, the gentle bulldog was bred especially to fight bulls. Its protruding mouth allowed it to hold onto the bull's throat while allowing the dog to breathe through the nose.) Fortunately, in 1824, the Royal Society for the Prevention of Cruelty to Animals was founded in England, specifically to put an end to these abuses. Forty-two years later, the Royal Society's American counterpart, the ASPCA, began to fight for the humane treatment of dogs in our country.

Dog Breeds

It's impossible to know for sure what breed of dog developed first. Wild dogs throughout the world bear a strong resemblance to one another. Domestic breeds, as we know, vary from the huge rottweiler to the tiny Pekingese. It is likely, though, that the first dogs were bred for their hunting abilities. An ancient piece of sculpture in Great Britain depicts Greek hero Alcibiades hunting with a dog that appears to be a modern Newfoundland.

Later, dogs were bred for size and ferocity to serve as watchdogs or for petite gentility to become lapdogs.

The very first classifications of dogs broke them down according to the shape of their skulls: elongated (hounds), moderately elongated (spaniels, setters, pointers), and having shortened muzzles (terriers and toy dogs). Shortly after the first dog show, held in Newcastle in 1859, the publication British Royal Sports published classifications of dogs based upon their uses:

"(a) Dogs that find game for man, leaving him to kill it himself—the pointers, setters, and spaniels. (b) Dogs which kill game when found for them—the English greyhound. (c) Dogs which find and also kill their game—the bloodhound, the foxhound, the harrier, the beagle. (d) Dogs which retrieve game that has been wounded by man—the retrievers. (e) Useful companions of man—the mastiff, the Newfoundland, the St. Bernard dog, the terriers, the bulldog, the dalmations. (f) Ladies' toy dogs."

It is on these classifications, and the first volume of the Kennel Stud Book published in 1874, that today's pedigree breeds are based.

Dog Terms

The 1913 Encyclopedia Britannica lists the following in its Glossary of Points of the Dog:

Apple Head: A rounded head, instead of a flat top.

Blaze: A white mark on the face.

Brisket: The part of the body in front of the chest.

Brush: The tail, usually applied to sheepdogs.

Butterfly Nose: A spotted nose.

Button Ear: When the tip falls over and covers the orifice.

Cat Foot: A short rounded foot, knuckles high and well developed.

Cheeky: When the cheek bumps are strongly defined.

Chops: The pendulous lip of the bulldog.

Cobby: Well ribbed-up, short and compact in proportion.

Couplings: Space between tops of shoulder blades and tops of hip joints.

Cow Hocks: Hocks that turn in.

Dew Claw: Extra claw, found occasionally on all breeds.

Dewlap: Pendulous skin under the throat.

Dish Faced: When nose is higher than muzzle at the top.

Dudley Nose: A yellow or flesh-colored nose.

Elbow: The joint at the top of the forearm.

Feather: The hair at the back of the legs and under the tail.

Flag: A term for the tail, applied to a setter.

Flews: The pendulous lips of the bloodhounds and St. Bernards.

Frill: A mass of hair on the chest, especially in collies.

Hare Foot: A long narrow foot, carried forward.

Haw: Red inside eyelid, shown in bloodhounds and St. Bernards.

Hucklebones: Tops of the hip bones.

Leather: The skin of the ear.

Occiput: The projecting bone or bump at the back of the head.

Overshot: The upper teeth projecting beyond the under.

Pig Jaw: Exaggeration of overshot.

Rose Ear: Where the tip of ear turns back, showing interior.

Smudge Nose: A nose which is not wholly black, but not spotted.

Stifles: The top joints of the hind legs.

Tulip Ear: An erect or pricked ear.

Undershot: The lower teeth projecting in front of the upper ones.

Dog Quotations

The dog was created specially for children. He is the god of frolic.

HENRY WARD BEECHER

Such fidelity of dogs in protecting what is committed to their charge, such affectionate attachment to their masters, such jealousy of strangers, such incredible acuteness of nose in following a track, such keenness in hunting — what else do they evince but that these animals were created for the use of man.

CICERO

Animals are such agreeable friends — they ask no questions; they pass no criticisms.

GEORGE ELIOT

There is no faith which has never yet been broken, except that of a truly faithful dog.

KONRAD Z. LORENZ

A dog's best friend is his illiteracy.

OGDEN NASH

A dog will never forget the crumb thou gavest him, though thou mayst afterwards throw a hundred stones at his head.

SA'DI

Buy a pup and your money will buy love unflinching.

RUDYARD KIPLING

The one absolutely unselfish friend that man can have in this selfish world, the one that never deserts him, the one that never proves ungrateful or treacherous, is his dog.

GEORGE G. VEST

If you are going to have a dog, first have a good dog; second, train it to be useful. It takes a little trouble to train a dog, maybe, but you will find that it more than pays in the end. It will give you a broader sympathy with the animal world, and that includes your fellow man.

HARRY J. MOONEY

No one appreciates the very special genius of your conversation as a dog does.

CHRISTOPHER MORLEY

Love me, love my dog.

SAINT BERNARD OF CLAIRVAUX

The great pleasure of a dog is that you may make a fool of yourself with him and not only will he not scold you, but he will make a fool of himself too.

SAMUEL BUTLER

I am his Highness' dog at Kew;
Pray tell me, sir, whose dog are you?

Inscription on a dog collar
given by Alexander Pope to his
Royal Highness

We are alone, absolutely alone on this chance planet, and, amid all the forms of life that surround us, not one, excepting the dog, has made an alliance with us.

MAURICE MAETERLINCK

There is no doubt that every healthy, normal boy (if there is such a thing in these days of Child Study) should own a dog at some time in his life, preferably between the ages of 45 and 50.

ROBERT BENCHLEY

Fox terriers are born with about four times as much original sin in them as in other dogs.

JEROME K. JEROME

Things that upset a terrier may pass virtually unnoticed by a Great Dane.

SMILEY BLANTON

The more I see of men, the better I like my dog.

FREDERICK THE GREAT

They say a reasonable amount o' fleas is good fer a dog — keeps him from broodin' over bein' a dog, mebbe.

EDWARD N. WESTCOTT

Watson: Is there any point to which you would wish to draw my attention?

Holmes: To the curious incident of the dog in the nighttime.

Watson: The dog did nothing in the nighttime.

Holmes: That was the curious incident.

SIR ARTHUR CONAN DOYLE,
Silver Blaze

If a dog's prayers were answered, bones would rain from the sky.

PROVERB

You ask of my companions. Hills, sir, and the sundown, and a dog as large as myself that my father bought me. They are better than beings, because they know, but do not tell.

EMILY DICKINSON

The best thing about a man is his dog.

FRENCH PROVERB

If dogs could talk, perhaps we would find it as hard to get along with them as we do with people.

KAREL CAPEK

When a man's best friend is his dog, that dog has a problem.

EDWARD ABBEY

If a dog will not come to you after he has looked you in the face, you should go home and examine your conscience.

WOODROW WILSON

Dogs like to obey. It gives them security.

JAMES HERRIOT

A Pekingese is not a pet dog; he is an undersized lion.

A. A. MILNE

Poodles always listen attentively while being scolded, looking innocent, bewildered, and misunderstood.

JAMES THURBER

I like a bit of mongrel myself, whether it's a man or a dog; it's the best for every day.

GEORGE BERNARD SHAW

Dachshunds are ideal dogs for small children, as they are already stretched and pulled to such a length that the child cannot do much harm one way or another.

ROBERT BENCHLEY

The nose of the bulldog has been slanted backward so that he can breathe without letting go.

WINSTON CHURCHILL

An Airedale can do anything any other dog can do and then whip the other dog if it has to.

THEODORE ROOSEVELT

The dog is the only living being that has found and recognizes an indubitable, tangible, and definite god. He knows to whom above him to give himself. He has not to seek for a superior and infinite power.

MAURICE MAETERLINCK

To be sure, the dog is loyal. But why, on that account, should we take him as an example? He is loyal to men, not to other dogs.

KARL KRAUS

Dogs are very different from cats in that they can be images of human virtue. They are like us.

IRIS MURDOCH

We see how he is at once in a world of smells of which we know nothing, which so occupy and absorb his attention as to make him practically blind to everything about him and deaf to all sounds, even to his master's voice impatiently calling him.

W. H. HUDSON

Dogs love company. They place it first in their short list of needs.

J. R. ACKERLEY

If you eliminate smoking and gambling, you will be amazed to find that almost all an Englishman's pleasures can be, and mostly are, shared by his dog.

GEORGE BERNARD SHAW

I would rather see the portrait of a dog that I know, than all the allegorical paintings they can show me in the world.

DR. JOHNSON

There are three faithful friends—an old wife, an old dog, and ready money.

BENJAMIN FRANKLIN

Those sighs of a dog! They go to the heart so much more deeply than the sighs of our own kind because they are utterly unintended, regardless of effect, emerging from one who, heaving them, knows not that they have escaped him!

JOHN GALSWORTHY

All knowledge, the totality of all questions and all answers, is contained in the dog.

FRANZ KAFKA

I love a dog. He does nothing for political reasons.

WILL ROGERS

Dogs

I've seen a look in dogs' eyes, a quickly vanishing look of amazed contempt, and I am convinced that dogs think humans are nuts.

JOHN STEINBECK

Barking dogs don't bite, but they themselves don't know it.

SHOLEM ALEICHEM

Histories are more full of examples of the fidelity of dogs than of friends.

ALEXANDER POPE

It breaks my heart to see stray dogs. . . . I don't believe in using physical force on dogs.

FRANK RIZZO

Dogs

It is fatal to let any dog know that he is funny,
for he immediately loses his head and starts
hamming it up.

P. G. WODEHOUSE

My dog is half pit bull, half poodle. Not much
of a watchdog, but a vicious gossip.

CRAIG SHOEMAKER

Dogs laugh, but they laugh with their tails.

MAX EASTMAN

Don't make the mistake of treating your dogs
like humans, or they'll treat you like dogs.

MARTHA SCOTT

Animals are not brethren, they are not underlings; they are other nations, caught with ourselves in the net of life and time.

HENRY BESTON

According to a recent survey conducted by Ralston Purina, the five most popular dog names in America are:

Duke

Brandy

Max

Sam

Shadow

Dog Stories

Mrs. Patrick Campbell was one of the most well-known actresses of the late Victorian and Edwardian eras, famous for her talents onstage and her wit off. Once, when leaving for a tour of North America, Mrs. Patrick Campbell attempted to smuggle her beloved Pekingese through customs by tucking it inside the upper part of her cape. "Everything was going splendidly," she recalled, "until my bosom barked."

Sir Winston Churchill owned a poodle named Rufus, who was an honored member of the prime minister's family. Each night at dinnertime, a special cloth was laid out for the dog on the Persian carpet beside Churchill's chair, and no one else would be served until Rufus had his meal.

Churchill often took Rufus with him when attending the movies. One night the pair went to see *Oliver Twist*. At the point in the movie when villain Bill Sykes was about to drown his dog in order to prevent the police from tracking him, Churchill covered Rufus's eyes with his hands and said, "Don't look now, dear! I'll tell you about it afterwards."

Hetty Green was a reclusive multimillionairess whose secretive ways and bad disposition earned her the nickname "the Witch of Wall Street." Hetty's most faithful friend was a dog that had the disturbing habit of biting her friends and visitors. Most people who encountered the dog said nothing about its bite, in fear that they would anger Hetty. Finally, one frequent victim of the dog's attacks said, "Hetty, that dog just bit me again! You've got to get rid of him!"

Hetty hugged the dog and said, "No, because he loves me, and he doesn't know how rich I am."

Radio director Tom Carlson, an admirer of the poet Ogden Nash, prized an autographed copy of one of Nash's books. Unfortunately, Carlson's dog chewed up the book shortly after it went out of print. After months of searching, Carlson managed to find another copy of the book, which he sent to Nash for an autograph. Nash returned it with the dedication: "To Tom Carlson or his dog — depending on whose taste it best suits."

British physicist Isaac Newton owned a prized dog named Diamond. One day the dog knocked over a candle on Newton's desk, and the resulting blaze destroyed many years' work. Upon discovering the destruction, Newton merely uttered, "O Diamond, Diamond, thou little knowest the damage thou hast done."

A black Newfoundland, Scannon, traveled with the Lewis and Clark expedition through the Louisiana Territory. On one occasion, according to Lewis's journal, Scannon saved the lives of three of the explorers by deflecting the charge of a rampaging buffalo. When the dog was later kidnapped by Indians, Lewis sent a search party to find the dog and kill its abductors. The dog was found abandoned by the Indians and rejoined the expedition unharmed.

Revolutionary French philosopher Jean-Jacques Rousseau had a pet dog named Duke. In his autobiography, *Confessions*, Rousseau wrote that his dog "was no beauty, but he certainly deserved the name [Duke] better than those who had assumed it."

Dog Heaven

You think dogs will not be in heaven? I tell you, they will be there long before any of us.

ROBERT LOUIS STEVENSON

Now thou art dead, no eye shall ever see,
For shape and service, Spaniell like to thee.
This shall my love doe, give thy sad death one
Teare, that deserves of me a million.

ROBERT HERRICK

Epitaph to a Newfoundland Dog

Near this spot

Are deposited the Remains of one

Who possessed Beauty without Vanity,

Strength without Insolence,

Courage without Ferocity,

And all the virtues of Man, without his Vices.

This Praise, which would be unmeaning

   Flattery

If inscribed over human ashes,

Is but a just Tribute to the Memory of

BOATSWAIN, a Dog,

Who was born at Newfoundland, May, 1803,
And died at Newstead Abbey, Nov. 18, 1808.

GEORGE GORDON, LORD BYRON

From *Bum*

So my good old pal, my irregular dog,
my flea-bitten, stub-tailed friend,
Has become a part of my very heart,
to be cherished till life-time's end:
And on Judgment Day, if I take the way
that leads where the righteous meet,
If my dog is barred by the heavenly guard
we'll both of us brave the heat!

W. DAYTON WEDGEFARTH

The poor dog, in life the firmest friend,

The first to welcome, foremost to defend,

Whose honest heart is still his master's own,

Who labours, fights, lives, breathes for him
alone,

Unhonour'd falls, unnoticed all his worth,

Denied in heaven the soul he held on earth.

While man, vain insect! hopes to be forgiven,

And claims himself a sole exclusive heaven.

GEORGE GORDON, LORD BYRON

According to Harper's Index, an estimated one million American dogs have been named as beneficiaries in wills.

The text of this book was set in Palatino by
Harry Chester, Inc. of New York, N.Y.

Design by Michael Mendelsohn